How to Make $100 a Month in the Stock Market

My method for getting house odds on Wall Street

By Eric Blair a.k.a.

The Onix Fox

TheOnixFox.com

Summed up Disclaimer: As much as I would love to be able to guarantee results for every trade, I can't. Some months I have lost money, but I win more often than I lose. A good tool or method doesn't exempt you from learning to perfect your craft.

Contents

Should you buy this book?

What if you could bet someone $100 that a stock won't be lower than it is today 1 month from now?

This book will explain how to do just that.

First let me make sure we are on the same page, so let's start with reasons NOT to buy this book...

1. If all you want is to get rich quick, or even within a couple years this is not it. I've tried to make this clear in the title; this is not a get rich quick plan.

2. If you think this will solve all your money problems. Again, it's simply what the title says it is, a way to make $100 a month and yes it's possible to make more, but what you do with any profits is up to you.

3. If you think this is a way for you to make money without learning anything or thinking at all: Sorry, you will still need a little brain power to do this. I will keep this as easy to understand as possible using examples and pictures as often as possible. I would venture to say that so long as you know the basic concept of insurance, that you pay a premium over a given time, and that you have protection from large loss. Also that the price of the insurance varies depending on how well protected you want to be, and for how long. If you can understand these basic concepts then keep reading.

4. If you believe what (friend/family/random person) told you about the stock market and that in one way or another they are all out to get you, it's rigged, ...can't win, ...big government conspiracy blah blah blah...

5. If you are well experienced in the market, especially in option strategies. This book probably

won't help you that much because its aim is for people new to the market, or specifically stock options.

6. If you already know everything. Yes, know-it-alls and haters please don't buy this book. You have to be able to learn a little, and not condemn something without trying it.

"Ridicule is the tribute paid to the genius by the mediocrities."
-Oscar Wilde

If any of these apply to you then, please don't buy this book I don't want your money enough to get negative reviews in the comments. Thank you for reading the sample and I truly hope you have a nice life regardless if you buy this or not. I've sold this method over 100 times so far as a test run, and have had only one person ask a question after I gave them my explanation of the method. That question was about an excel spreadsheet I added to help figure the risk versus reward ratio. I hope this means that I am decently good at explaining this method to people.

How much to get started?
"When I was young I thought that money was the most important thing in life; now that I am old I know that it is."
-Oscar Wilde

The first question most people ask me about this method is "How much money do I need to start with?" It's a great question, and it was mine as well. First you need enough to meet the minimum requirements for the broker you choose, not just the minimum balance to open an account, but also to be able to have what's known as a "margin account" (if you already know what a margin account is, don't panic my method does not require borrowing money).

For those that don't know what a margin account is I will explain in more detail later. So far the brokers I've seen require $2,000.00, I want to be upfront about this. If you have this much to start with great. If you don't and you think that it's impossible to get this much in your current circumstances, then please don't buy this book because I don't want you to feel I misled you. I have read several books where the minimum amount recommended to start trading was several chapters in, and most books quoted $20,000 to start, not $2,000.

I must stress any money you fund your account with CANNOT be money you need for your monthly expenses, or money that you cannot live without

To get started it might mean waiting for the next tax return or cut back and save up. For me it has been well worth it for the monthly income I make with this method.

So far I have only traded in U.S. markets. I have not traded commodities or currencies. I will say this, while other market's options may be in different amounts and have different rules; I was first inspired to get into stock option trading from listening to an interview of David Novac by Robert Kiyosaki. David Novac trades the Australian market so the method I explain should work in other markets but as of this writing I have no experience in these other markets.

Feel free to skip to the next chapter if you wish, but I had to share this experience as to why my friends describe me as "tenacious" when learning about the stock market and trading. Where most books either assume you know a lot more, or are just really dry I hope I haven't learned so much that this book falls into that category.

The best motivational speech given to me!

I'm having an out of body experience, I can see myself standing in front of one of my managers at my first "real" job my sophomore year in high school (McDonalds). I'm hot and sweaty after only a 5 hour shift working in front of the grill, and the uniform they gave me had a permanent grease smell that I found out never comes out... ever. I had put in my 2 weeks' notice a few days ago because I wasn't getting enough hours there to afford my crappy first truck. Belinda was explaining to me how to get more hours and that the secret was to "really strive to get that McChicken up there"...

I honestly wanted to say "did you really just that!?" I wasn't the slowest employee, but did she think I was going to start sprinting the meat patty's off the grill to the dressing station for minimum wage? I thought we had an established agreement; you get a minimum wage slave because nobody hires high school kids for more than that and I get a little money to buy a car, insurance and a little money to blow on girls. That's how it worked, right!? But then I began to feel sorry for her and then I said a silent prayer

"Dear God I don't know what will happen to me in the next 25 years, but before I'm put in a position to attempt to convince a high school kid to give 110% for a fast food restaurant when I'm over 40 please smite me dead with a lightning bolt, because I've failed at life and am not happy. Thank you for your time, Amen"

If that sounds overly harsh, or offensive to anybody working fast food please don't be offended and understand my meaning, there is nothing wrong with fast food heck McDonalds (MCD) is a publicly traded stock part of the Dow Jones Industrial Average. I would work there again if I had to, to make ends meet, but not longer than I needed to and if I were a manager in her position I would try to level with the kid. "Look man I know it's not your life's ambition to work the grill for the rest of your life, but try to keep things moving and I'll make sure to give a great reference when you get a real job. Oh and here is a book on how to make $100 a month in the stock market."

Who to Trade with: Picking a Broker in 3 steps

Step 1: Pick an on-line broker that you like (obviously if you already have a broker skip to the next step). This is a personal preference I use Etrade, and am considering using TDameritrade as well. I've have considered Trade king, Options House, and OptionsExpress but haven't tested them out as of this writing. Do your homework and pick one that you think will be the best fit for you, like so many things most of the time you get the service you pay for.

Step 2: You need to fund your account (again with money you don't depend on) most brokers have several ways to do this: check, transfer, etc.

Step 3: You need to get permission from the broker you have selected to trade options, including what is called a "Credit Spread" or tell your broker that you need to be able to trade these also known as "Bull Put" spreads or the reverse "Bear Call". Some brokers will allow you to apply on-line for permission to trade options, they have to show you a document (by law) to read over so you know what you are getting into.

Side note: quite honestly getting permission from your broker is not difficult but may be the more annoying part. When I applied on-line for permission to trade stock options I ended up having to call my broker to give more details of what type of trading I wanted to do. My broker had option trading split up into 4 different levels (I don't know if other brokers do this the same way). The first level only allowed "Covered Calls" I'm not going to explain this method in this book, but it's not what I was looking for. The second level lets you trade individual options, also helpful but only on level 3 was where I could trade my method I teach in this book. Option level 4 is for another type of trade I'm not going to cover in this book either, that involves what's called selling "naked options" this is NOT for beginners! Or some people altogether.

Here is where the "Margin" account comes in, there is a good chance your broker will require you to open this type of account. Margin is simply a line of credit. It works like this, if you have $2000 in your account you can buy up to $4000 worth of stock, and like any line of credit they charge you interest. Don't worry my method does not require or recommend that you borrow money.

Three steps and you are up and ready to trade. An important concept about brokers in general is that you should never be afraid to call them with questions or concerns, because they are providing you a service. So long as you keep trading they keep making money on commissions, this should be a win/win partnership. So, if you get a bad feeling pick another broker.

What to trade: Options

"Anyone who stops learning is old, whether at twenty or eighty. Anyone who keeps learning stays young. The greatest thing in life is to keep your mind young."

-Henry Ford

"Wealth is the product of man's capacity to think."

-Ayn Rand

For some this is going to be the biggest learning section, if you already know what a stock option is then head to the next chapter <u>What to Trade: ETF</u>.

Instead of buying stocks themselves, I trade stock options. A stock option is simply a contract between a buyer and a seller of a stock. It gives one person the right to either buy or sell at a specific price by a specific time.

There are two types of options. Ones that give the right to buy the stock are named "Call" options. And options that give the right to sell a stock are called "Put" options.

They both have two Characteristics
1. A **"Strike Price"** is price of the stock you can use the option at for call options the right to buy, and for put options the right to sell.
2. An **expiration date** is just what it sounds like. Just like coupons and term insurance expires, call and put options expire as well.

Call Example: Let's say your friend is selling a TV for $200 and you tell them you want to buy it but won't have the cash until payday. Your friend tells you that they will sell it to you for $100 so long as you have the cash by payday, but if you back out, they'll put it up on craigslist. Now, most friends I know wouldn't do this, but in this case the friend asks you to give him $20 to hold it for you and he gets to keep it whether or not you end up buying it. So, if you back out you are out the $20, but if you buy the TV your total cost is $120.

This is how a "Call" option works, your specified price is the "strike price" and the "expiration date" is payday.

Put Example: Put options are similar to insurance, or a warranty where if you buy a TV for $300 from a store and at the register they ask if you would like a year warranty for $20. This is similar to a "Put" option. The "strike price" is the cost of the TV $300, the "expiration date" is one year away.

Call and Put Pricing Example: The price you pay for your options depends on their value and both characteristics determine their value. Just like a warranty how long it covers and for how much of the original price determines its value.

So if you ask your friend to wait 2 months to buy his TV they might ask you to give them $40 to hold it. The store might offer you a 2 year warranty for $50.

The value compared to the current price is a little different since normally the store won't offer you a warranty for more than the value of the TV like saying you can get $350 back if it breaks within a year but that warranty costs $100. But with options you can do that, or get less protection for cheaper like getting $200 back on a $300 TV if you only spend $10. So with options you get well... more options or choices if you prefer.

Option amounts:
In America, options are bought and sold in packs of 100, but the price is always shown for the individual option (not the pack of 100). So, if you want to buy an option that shows a cost of $0.50 you have to buy 100 at a time, so this would cost you $50.00.

Stock & Option Example
If you bought 100 shares of Amazon stock and if it was currently trading at $101.00 you could buy put options to have the right to sell your stock at $100 (strike price).

So if you bought these today, and tomorrow bad news comes out and your Amazon stock drops half to $50 you can still have the right to sell yours for $100, the strike price that you bought your options for.
Now if the option expires and the stock never goes back under $100 then your options that you bought expires worthless. Just like term life insurance, you pay a premium whether something bad happens or not, but if it does happen you are not hurting so bad.

The "Call" option is the right to buy a stock, so it's more like buying a coupon. An example would be if you bought a call option on Apple when it was trading at $200, and used (or exercised) the option when Apple moved up to selling at $300. You would only pay the $200 strike price for the stock when it's worth $300, minus only the price you paid for the call option and your broker's commission fee.

Now, as soon as you get you head wrapped around this concept, I don't know about you, but I was blown away. I was so excited, but also annoyed no one told me before. I think I actually yelled "WHY THE CRAP DIDN'T THEY TEACH ME THIS IN HIGH SCHOOL!?" it almost made me sick to think about how many people could have protected their investments during crashes.

So to recap, "Put" options are like insurance, and "Call" options are like coupons. If you want to protect your investment buy put options, if you have reason to believe a company is going to do great by curing cancer or inventing something amazing, buy call options. Or, if you just want to buy and sell options instead of stock you can do that too. If you think it's going up, buy a call. If you think it's going down, buy a put. If nothing else this allows you to be able to make money if the market goes up or down! Instead of just being able to buy stock hoping it goes up.

Just wait it gets better. Options enable new strategies that buying stock doesn't allow. But before that, I have to show you what I trade.

What to Trade: ETF

"I have never let my schooling interfere with my education"

-Mark Twain

The hard part should be over. Once you have your account ready to trade options and you start to understand options. You'll need to pick what stock or in my case, ETF (exchange traded fund) that you want to trade.

One of the main advantages is that drastic movements (referred to as volatility) should be less often and that is good for the way we want to trade. Here is a list of American ETF's...
http://en.wikipedia.org/wiki/List_of_American_exchange-traded_funds
I prefer ETF's that are based on market indexes like the DOW (DIA), NASDAQ (QQQ), Russell2000 (IWM), and S&P500 (SPY). However these are a fraction of the cost, 1/100th of the price of buying shares of the Dow Jones Industrial Average (DJIAD is the index stock symbol).
Ok, time to clarify a few things. If you are anything like me when I started, I didn't know what the DOW was (or most commonly Dow Jones Industrial Average DJIA). It's simply 30 stocks grouped together here is a list on Market Watch
(http://www.marketwatch.com/investing/index/DJIA).

Many people that have contacted me, already have an idea of either a specific stock or sector of the market they want to invest in. This is great! But be warned, not all stocks have stock options to trade, and some don't have enough volume of options to be safe to trade.

You will want to trade stocks that have a lot of options available to trade above and below the strike price, this is called "open interest" on option charts. Some stocks or ETF's have so many options that they even have options that expire weekly, not just monthly like most (third Friday of the month). Here is a screenshot of some options that don't have a lot of "open interest" a few are in the hundreds but some have only 10 or 11. If nothing else, it means there are not a lot of opportunities to buy options. Don't get overwhelmed by the other numbers, this page is referred to as an "options chain" if you look in the middle they are sorted by strike price. Call options are on the left and Put options are on the right, like any EBay auction, they have a bid and an ask price. While I'm on the subject of bid and ask prices, you want these prices to be as close as possible. This is called a "spread" or "Bid Ask Spread". Making this another example of a stock you would not want to trade options with because the spread is so wide.

				CALLS						AUG 21 '15				PUTS					
Trade	Quote	Open Interest	Volume	Net Change	Last	Bid	Ask	Strike Price	Bid	Ask	Last	Net Change	Volume	Open Interest	Quote	Trade
Trade	Details	6	0	0.00	1.68	1.05	1.40	2.50	0.00	0.10	0.00	0.00	0	0	Details	Trade
Trade	Details	25	0	0.00	0.04	0.00	0.05	5.00	1.15	1.50	0.00	0.00	0	0	Details	Trade
Trade	Details	0	0	0.00	0.00	0.00	0.10	7.50	3.50	4.00	0.00	0.00	0	0	Details	Trade

Closing Price August 14, 2015 4:02:00 PM EDT   In the money

This is from MarketWatch.com where you can start to look at options chains and get familiar with what they look like. You can also look at them on finance.yahoo.com or several other sites.

At the time of this writing, I exclusively trade either SPY, DIA, IWM, or QQQ because of the leverage I mentioned that it's less likely or less often that any index would move quickly up or down, such as when earnings reports come out. For the method I'm going to explain in the next chapter, we want nice and steady movements when possible. Even though the method gives you good odds, but you want house odds and the house looks for as many ways as possible to increase your chance of payout.

Earnings explained: Earnings are the net benefits of a corporation's operation. For a more detailed description check the Wiki here http://en.wikipedia.org/wiki/Earnings I generally don't look for earnings as a way to make trades, so I don't normally concern myself with them, but it's important to know that the price of stocks can change drastically and often less predictably when earnings are reported.

How to Trade: The Method

"You don't get paid for what you do, you get paid for what you know."

-Murph

You might or might not get this step right away. If not don't worry, just keep going and if you don't pick it up the first time it will start to make more sense the more you go over it. Trust me when I say, the probability this trading method offers is well worth the learning curve.

Now, hopefully you're starting to grasp the concept of what Stock Options are, the method is normally referred to as a "credit spread". This can be done for up "bull market" or down "bear market" trades. The majority of the time the market goes up more than it goes down, so you'll probably use put options most of the time (the insurance not the coupon), and will be for most of the examples I give.

You'll sell put options with a strike price below what the stock or ETF is currently trading, (I'll cover more on how far down I pick strike prices later). Next you will buy an equal number of options you sold, only these options strike price will be lower than the strike price of the options you sold. It will look like this.

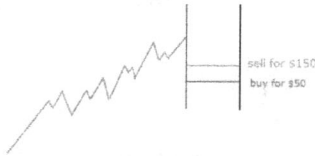

In this example, I wrote that the price you sell the options for is $150, and the ones you buy for are $50. Thus, you have your $100 and the black lines represent time about 1 or 2 months. One thing I thought was very interesting was that you take in your profit at the very start of the trade!

So basically what you have done is sold insurance and bought a cheaper insurance to protect yourself, so long as the stock/ETF stays above the strike price of the options you sold (top red line) you keep your $100. Different things can happen in that month obviously the best case scenario is this.

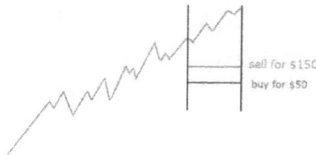

It's also fun to know that if the stock doesn't do much at all, but hangs around the same price you can keep the same max profit of $100. Unlike if you had bought low with the goal of selling high in a normal stock or option.

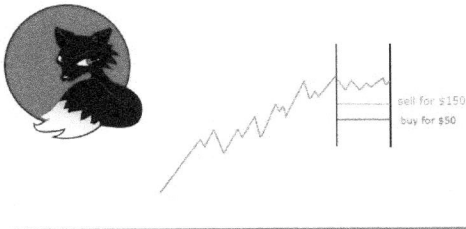

You even have some wiggle room if the stock goes down a little.

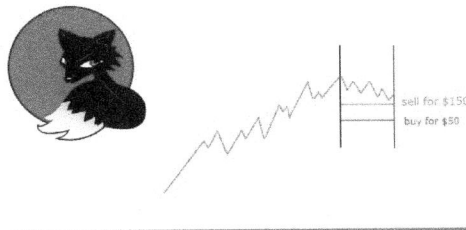

Of course nothing is perfect and sometimes this can happen.

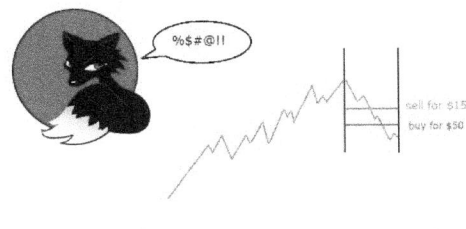

The solution is to get out of the trade by buying back what you sold and selling what you bought (a little confusing I know but it will make more sense the more you work with it).

Like most things trading can be simple, but not always easy. Eating healthy consistently is simple but not easy.

In the case of stocks the best example being when something like this happens.

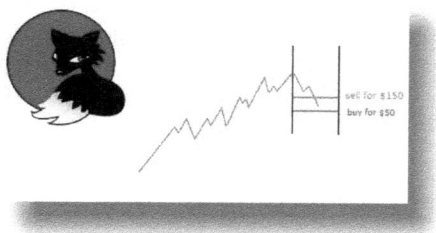

The big question is should you get out? You still have time for it to go up and you hope it will like this.

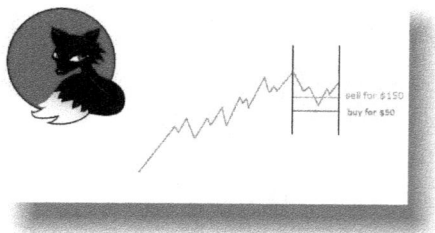

This has happened to me, but from my experience it's a bad practice. You want to get out before it crosses the price you sold options at. This can result in a loss, but in my experience it's not worth the risk to stay in.

The better choice is to get out and either open another trade lower than before or open a trade in the opposite direction (using Call options) if you think it will continue down.

Like I said before, the market in general moves up more than it moves down, but when it does move down it normally moves faster down. A common phrase is "the Bull goes up the stairs and the Bear jumps out the window".

Why This Method: Psychology

"I am an old man and have known a great many troubles, but most of them never happened."

-Mark Twain

Entire books have been written about trading psychology and for good reason. It's probably the largest factor in becoming a good trader long term. I'm focusing this chapter on the benefits and tips for this specific method and I recommend reading Mark Douglas' book "Trading in the Zone" to cover Trading Psychology more completely.

Most people I know hate losing more than they enjoy winning, even though that may seem like the same thing. I can think of several times I've had a win at something in life that seemed huge before I did it, but then after it wasn't as big of a deal. Then on the flip side, had a fail that was big enough to throw myself a pity party.

With that in mind even though this might seem to be a more complex strategy for a beginner, I still think the learning curve is absolutely worth it because of the ways it keeps you off an emotional roller coaster that comes with trading, especially for beginners.

5 frustrations that are avoided by using this method

- **Frustration** - Selling your stock just to see it keep going up.
  - ✓ **Avoided** - With this method your max profit is fixed.
- **Frustration** - Buying a stock and seeing it go down.

- ✓ **Avoided** - So long as you open your trade out of the money like I recommend you should have some wiggle room for downward movement before you would have to exit at a large loss, so you have a little time for it to go your way.
- **Frustration** - Buying a stock and watch it do nothing.
  - ✓ **Avoided** - with this trade if it's doesn't move much for the whole month, you still keep your max profit.
- **Frustration** – Stressing over every little market tick.
  - ✓ **Avoided** – If the stock moves up or not at all, or even down a little you can still keep your whole profit. So long as it doesn't go too far down. Small market moves won't affect you nearly as much, and after several trades maybe not at all.
- **Frustration** – Commission fees are annoying.
  - ✓ **Partially avoided** – If the options expire, you don't have to pay a second commission fee to close the trade.

Test for free, then start trading small
Prove that the method works by taking a screenshot of the price of options (also known as an option chain)

Then, follow up when those options expire, basically a fake trade with no money risked.

When you are ready to trade, start small and with low risk by starting far out of the money but enough to still get a profit. In the next chapter I cover seasonality's of the market so you can get started when the market is historically strong. You can get better prices if your options expire 2-3 months away.

Aug 21 '15		Aug 28 '15w		Sep 4 '15w		Sep 11 '15w		Sep 18 '15	>	All Months

		CALLS						SEP 18 '15		PUTS						
Trade	Quote	Open Interest	Volume	Net Change	Last	Bid	Ask	Strike Price	Bid	Ask	Last	Net Change	Volume	Open Interest	Quote	Trade
Trade	Details	31,548	1,433	0.49	6.29	6.26	6.38	205.00	2.09	2.13	2.11	-0.41	53,142	208,399	Details	Trade
Trade	Details	17,815	1,496	0.42	5.45	5.48	5.60	206.00	2.36	2.41	2.40	-0.43	12,661	66,170	Details	Trade
Trade	Details	21,287	8,037	0.47	4.77	4.74	4.84	207.00	2.67	2.72	2.67	-0.49	5,381	57,481	Details	Trade
Trade	Details	28,298	4,398	0.36	4.06	4.01	4.13	208.00	3.02	3.03	3.08	-0.47	18,414	90,690	Details	Trade
Trade	Details	38,454	8,739	0.37	3.40	3.36	3.45	209.00	3.39	3.43	3.38	-0.58	6,139	60,603	Details	Trade
Trade	Details	88,470	14,095	0.28	2.76	2.74	2.78	210.00	3.77	3.86	3.85	-0.61	5,128	94,415	Details	Trade
Trade	Details	99,110	8,588	0.24	2.19	2.17	2.22	211.00	4.30	4.38	4.36	-0.57	1,540	34,231	Details	Trade
Trade	Details	62,756	5,805	0.18	1.68	1.66	1.71	212.00	4.78	4.93	4.90	-0.70	858	36,468	Details	Trade
Trade	Details	63,104	3,272	0.15	1.25	1.22	1.27	213.00	5.39	5.62	5.54	-0.75	860	27,474	Details	Trade

Rule number 1

Even more important than not talking about fight club is to **cut losses quickly** so they don't become large losses. This is simple, but not easy because of your emotions. **Emotions are your enemy! Logic is your friend!**

This is already a high probability trade, so the odds will ever be in your favor. However nothing works 100% of the time.

The solution is a stop loss.

This is not the Pirate code! It's not a guideline, it's a rule! Set a firm price to exit the trade and stick with it. In fact, you should write it down before even getting in the trade. Being able to do this consistently might be the one key of success for your trading because most people don't have the discipline.

Where to set a stop loss completely depends on your tolerance for risk. I can't tell you what is best for you, but I would not let the stock price pass below the strike price of the options you sold. I would say a good minimum is around a dollar away from the strike price.

Failing to get out can result in larger losses and set you back several months if you are not careful. Some people have decided they are done and never trade again.

Getting out early can work to profit as well sometimes

One month I was fortunate enough to have a trade make 50% of the total profit I wanted to make in just a week, I took my profits and placed another similar trade with the same expiration date just to see it do it again in another week and a half. I had made 100% of a trade that I set up for a month away, but did it in just over half the time.

This type of trading makes me feel like I'm on the dealer side of a Roulette table, in that you start with money placed on your table (in your account), the odds are in your favor and all you have to do is wait for the wheel to stop and 2/3 of the wheel are profitable for you.

How you trade is up to you, whether you get out when you make 25% or 50% or wait for your options to expire. For me, I get a personal high when I'm able to profit from the options expiring, I feel like the one time I bowled 4 strikes in a row (2 turkeys).

Perspective can remove some fear

Different date ranges can change your perspective. If the stock moves down sharply enough to shake you, keep in mind your stop loss. So long as it's below a simple moving average like the 50day or 100day simple moving average, you can change the chart to show the last 3 or 6 months and it can help your perspective drastically.

Remember the method can be reversed for bear market

So far, I've assumed your trades would be put options to make money in a Bull (upward) Market. The method can be reversed by using Call options above the stock price if you think or see the market moving down. Keep in mind that the market generally moves down quicker than it moves up, so this is probably something you want to be ready to get out of quicker as well if need be.

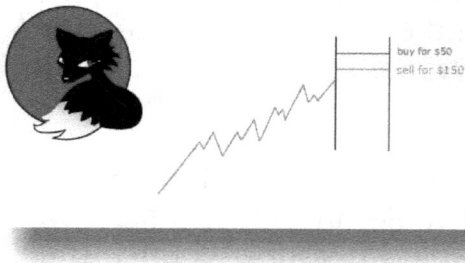

Loss

If and or when you experience a loss in a trade, and you are angry or stressed do not get right back in another trade! Take a walk with deep breaths, and remind yourself nothing works 100% of the time. Only return when you have calmed down and are not angry and insistent on getting "your" money back right away. That's why it's best to get out fast with a small loss not a large one, you kick yourself harder and longer the bigger the loss... trust me on this, I know from experience.

Anger, greed, and fear can encourage you to make snap decisions or convince yourself of patterns or indicators. When you can trade without emotion, you can get back in. Even if this means waiting a day or two or longer especially if you decide you only want to

trade the market one direction (up or down/Bull or Bear).
You need to become like a Jedi, emotions exist but they don't affect you.

"Fear is the path to the dark side…fear leads to anger…anger leads to hate…hate leads to suffering."

–Yoda

When to Trade: Trends

"October. This is one of the peculiarly dangerous months to speculate in stocks. The others are July, January, September, April, November, May, March, June, December, August, and February."

-Mark Twain

One of the best books I've read is the "Stock Market Almanac" by Jeffrey A. Hirsch, it has all kinds of trends that have been going on in the market since 1950. One of the bigger ones that caught my attention is a 6 month pattern of the DOW. Most years from November 1st to April 30 is the 6 good months of the DOW, then from May 1st to October 30th is the bad or less predictable 6 months of the DOW.

The great thing is you can go to several websites and look back at historical charts and see this for yourself, even in the crash of 2008 losses would have been significantly reduced if you followed this pattern.

As you can see the market was already down, but as of May 1st it didn't do its worst for another few months.

The almanac goes on to say that when used with the MACD indicator (I'll cover in the next chapter) it is even more effective.

If you look at different years, you can see that even during the bad/weak months it can still go up. 2013 for example looks almost too perfect and that's why I call it less predictable instead of just bad.

Where to Trade: Technical Indicators

"Shallow men believe in luck. Strong men believe in cause and effect."

-Ralph Waldo Emerson

Everything before this has been how the method works. The following will be the indicators that will help you decide where to place the trades or how far away from the strike price you want to be.

Simple moving averages (SMA) are just what you might think, an average price of a stock over a specified amount of days. 20, 50, 100 etc.

For me just placing moving averages on the same chart, I start to think of rules to trade by. Such as opening a trade when the stock goes above all the averages then get out if it touches the top average.

Support and Resistance lines, these are much more subjective and are generally not drawn on charts automatically, you have to do it manually (if your software allows it). Put simply these are points of commonality over a given time and are horizontal, and simply show how stocks have trouble breaking up through resistance lines and/or dropping below support lines. All of them can be broken but it's all to show you what is likely or unlikely of where a stock will stop. When broken they can often switch, where broken resistance lines become support and vice versa.

This is supply and demand at its core, prices people are willing to buy and sell at. They can often form around round numbers, people tend to set stop losses at support lines.

MACD (Moving Average Convergence Divergence) this has been most consistently favored indicator that I have read about, and its main purpose is to determine the current trend and changes of trend.

The changes of direction are made clear by the lines crossing. Nothing is perfect, but this and the moving averages are my favorites. With heavy consideration of Support and Resistance lines.

Bollinger Bands are awesome and were a heavy influence when I set up my trades early on. Methods of trading intended by the creator John Bollinger can be found right on his site (http://www.bollingerbands.com/). The outer bands expand and contract with Volatility. I use them as guides to supplement support or resistance levels. While I have a great amount of respect for these and their creator, they are mathematically over my head and I trudged through the creator's entire book talking about the math and how they came to be, just to find out that the methods to trade with them are on his site for free (last time I looked anyway).

RSI (Relative Strength Index) is another indicator I like, but I haven't found a way to help set up entering or exiting rules that I prefer yet using this indicator. Another author I like said he waits for RSI to be at an extreme on either side before he gets into credit spreads. I'm not entirely certain if these would be better to help you trade with a trend or find the trend changes.

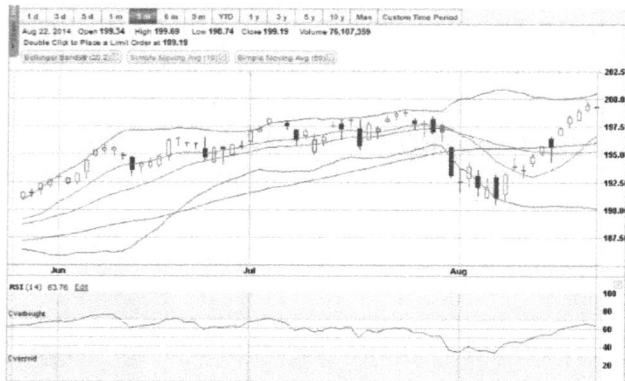

Most people trade one of two different ways; trend following, or contrarily meaning they trade expecting it to change directions. A common phrase I've often read is "The trend is your friend" or "The trend is your friend, until the end". I would say these are probably what you should keep in mind while looking for places to enter a trade. For beginners going with the trend would probably be best, because you are only wrong if it changes direction and comes too close to the options you have sold. When a trend already exists you can generally see it, so for me at least trying to predict when it's going to change is more difficult.

How to be a Pro: 3 keys

"Be at war with your vices, at peace with your neighbors, and let every New Year find you a better man."

-Benjamin Franklin

From all the books I've read and my experiences, three things separate a beginner from a pro.

1. Pros have a trading plan written down on paper.
2. Pros regularly review past trades to see what works most.
3. Pros follow their plan even if it means the trade loses money. If the plan is good the war is won even if the battle is lost.

After you get some trades under your belt, you need to figure out how you react to situations by keeping a log. You might find that you can get a feel for timing on Bearish trades. Or you might decide that it's too stressful, and you want to stick with Bull moves. If one way of trading you find easier not to break your rules then stick with it.

How to look at losses

By three methods we may learn wisdom: First, by reflection, which is noblest; second, by imitation, which is easiest; and third by experience, which is the bitterest.

-Confucius

Sometimes life hits you in the head with a brick. Don't lose faith.

-Steve Jobs

If you should be trading and break your rules and suffer a large loss at some point, despite your best efforts you need to do a self-examination to think about what influences your decisions.

I have done this, I've broken my rules and let the stock fall past the options I sold and I kept holding onto it because it was in the 6 good months and the moving averages had not crossed. I thought it would come back up but eventually I had to get out and it hurt my ego and my account badly.

To make matters worse, the trade itself was for several months long. I had been very aggressive in the strike price selection. I think I was more upset about losing the time and opportunity for making money, thinking about how much I could have made if I had followed smaller trends and took profits out sooner. So yes, it was about the money and possible money made but I had also lost time which is more valuable.

If this happens to you, you need to decide if you will learn from your mistake and count the loss as the cost of education or keep trading and risk making the same mistake, or quit altogether. This is why I highly recommend both writing the rules down on paper and keeping a record and reviewing your progress. Look closely at your winners and at your losers to see what you can learn.

"If you know the enemy and know yourself you need not fear the results of a hundred battles."

-Sun Tzu

Cash can be a position, if you are too emotional to trade DON'T! Or if you don't see a trend of any kind and are not comfortable just sit with your cash and wait for something you are comfortable with.

To further help your outlook on losing trades, you might try thinking of every trade as an employee of your business. When you have a trade do badly you, fire it. If that seems too harsh in your mind, think of it as a contractor or service provider of some kind that you just won't hire again.

The key being that you must try to emotionally distance yourself from it. Your ego cannot be tied to every trade because you will hold on longer than you want. Even if it works out by holding on to it, it's not good practice because you can get hurt, you will start to think that you can do no wrong. Each employee (trade) has a resume of indicators the MACD or 6 months of the DOW, moving average, etc...

Remember as soon as you get out of the trade you can get immediately in another if you want, but remember "Cash is a position" if you are not sure your emotions are in check, maybe wait until you feel comfortable with which way the market is going.

"Failure is simply the opportunity to begin again, this time more intelligently."

-Henry Ford

I don't know that everybody should trade but everyone should at least have their money working for them for retirement, I plan to write my next book to cover this more, signup to receive my emails to find out when it and any other books or video series are coming out.

Know what the risk and rewards

Calculating the risk verses reward can be a little complicated, I normally use an excel sheet that I set up to manage running the numbers quickly for me. I'll show you how to do the same or have a calculator or both on my website.

We start by finding the awesome part, the profit. You take the price of options sold minus price of options bought then times 100 (because options are sold in 100 at a time in the American markets). In the example you would take $0.87-$0.39 = $0.48. Then take your $0.48 x 100 = $48.00 so your profit from this would be $48 if you sold 3 and bought three options the profit would be $144 (voila $100 in a month). Just to be clear this is not an example of a trade I would recommend it's just an example to show the calculation.

$$(0.87-0.39) \times 100 = 48$$

It's not all sunshine and roses, now it's time to calculate the risk. Which will actually be more than the profit which can be a frightening thought. Just keep two things in mind, first being this is a High Probability trade, 2/3 conditions keep you profitable. The second thing to keep in mind, is that you are not locked in this trade, if you get uncomfortable you can close this trade by buying back what you sold, and selling what you bought.

Risk is calculated by getting the difference between the strike prices (170-168) then times 100, and then subtracting your profit.

(170-168) x 100 – 48 = 152

And if you did three of these...
48 x 3 = 144 profit
152 x 3 = 456 risk

		CALLS						SEP 20 '14				PUTS				
Trade	Quote	Open Interest	Volume	Net Change	Last	Bid	Ask	Strike Price	Bid	Ask	Last	Net Chan	Volume	Open Interest	Quote	Trade
Trade	Details	4,935	70	0.57	2.72	2.61	2.82	168.00	0.38	0.39	0.38	-0.19	407	3,894	Details	Trade
Trade	Details	455	10	0.30	1.97	2.19	2.36	168.50	0.46	0.47	0.51	-0.29	137	1,398	Details	Trade
Trade	Details	3,871	197	0.08	1.62	1.78	1.91	169.00	0.57	0.58	0.58	-0.24	1,440	3,842	Details	Trade
Trade	Details	442	108	0.27	1.40	1.39	1.45	169.50	0.70	0.71	0.69	-0.32	383	909	Details	Trade
Trade	Details	27,165	983	0.21	1.04	1.06	1.07	170.00	0.87	0.89	0.89	-0.36	645	4,891	Details	Trade
Trade	Details	2,155	410	0.12	0.72	0.74	0.75	170.50	1.09	1.10	1.99	-0.41		1,896	Details	Trade
Trade	Details	2,423	328	0.14	0.51	0.48	0.49	171.00	1.35	1.40	1.40	-0.32	328	2,774	Details	Trade
Trade	Details	1,156	63	0.06	0.28	0.28	0.29	171.50	1.59	1.76	1.96	-0.47	77	607	Details	Trade
Trade	Details	8,268	372	0.04	0.15	0.14	0.15	172.00	1.95	2.24	2.50	-0.13	6	828	Details	Trade
Trade	Details	2,210	36	0.02	0.06	0.06	0.08	172.50	2.35	2.80	2.89	-0.60	12	91	Details	Trade
Trade	Details	1,784	101	0.00	0.02	0.02	0.03	173.00	2.84	3.25	3.85	0.00	0	370	Details	Trade

Real Time September 15, 2014 2:53:00 PM EDT

That is about as clear as I can make it on paper, and that's why I have excel do it for me, plus a few more calculations I like to look at. It's one of the 2 things I never trade without.

Looking at these numbers should help you decide whether or not to get in a trade and at what price. Remember, it's a good idea to start free and start small. Don't compare yourself to other people on this, your risk tolerance may be different from other people you want to trade with a low enough risk that you can sleep at night. That's no joke!

Remember, a successful trade is one you follow your rules, not so much if it's profitable or not. I know that sounds backwards or crazy even but if you follow your rules, then as long as you have a good system you will win more often and make more than you lose.

In Closing

"The secret of getting ahead is getting started."

-Mark Twain

"Whether you think that you can, or that you can't, you are usually right."

-Henry Ford

Congratulations for making it through my book and thank you! You are now 1000 times more equipped than I was when I started.

This method is a tool like a hammer, a hammer can be used to drive nails in boards to build a house or it can smash holes in drywall and windows to tear it down. It's all in how wisely you use the tools you have and now you have a new tool.

I had to resist throwing everything I've learned in this book, but I realized that a lot of it is not necessary to get started, so I've tried to keep this to the basics to what you need to get started, and leave any other details to those who ask for them by signing up for my emails.

"It's not the daily increase but daily decrease. Hack away at the unessential."

-Bruce Lee

For some people making the first trade can seem intimidating, and the longer you wait the harder it gets like jumping off the diving board. If you find that this is you, I'd like you to read one of my favorite teacher's favorite quote.

"It is not the critic who counts, not the man who points out how the strong man stumbled, or where the doer of deeds could have done better. The credit belongs to the man who is actually in the arena; whose face is marred by the dust and sweat and blood; who strives valiantly; who errs and comes short again and again, because there is no effort without error or shortcoming; who knows the great enthusiasms, the great devotions and spends himself in a worthy cause; who at the best, knows in the end the triumph of high achievement, and who, at worst, if he fails, at least fails while daring greatly; so that his place shall never be with those cold and timid souls who know neither victory or defeat."

-Theodore Roosevelt

Contact me

Thank you for buying and reading my book, I hope it's a blessing to you. If you would like to learn another way to trade similar to this method, or want examples showing how I doubled my money in 2014 using this method, and the 2 things I don't trade without subscribe to my email list.

http://TheOnixFox.com

For quick updates follow me on Twitter
http://twitter.com/EricBlair2024

www.ingramcontent.com/pod-product-compliance
Lightning Source LLC
Chambersburg PA
CBHW070921210326

41521CB00010B/2265